Confidently You

Confidently You

21-DAY ACTION PLAN TO YOUR PROFESSIONAL BEST

———

Michele Badie

Confidently You, 21-Day Action Plan to Your Professional Best

ISBN-13: 9780692678053
ISBN-10: 0692678050
Library of Congress Control Number: 2016906994
Sylvia M Badie, Altamonte Springs, FL

Dedication

"Go confidently in the direction of your dreams. Live the life you've imagined."

-Henry David Thoreau

Brittney Rashawn
Jazmin La'Rae
Kiarie Aimetria
Morgan Jenae
Morgan Simone
Nicholas Jay
Shacara Antonette
Sonali Anya

Gratitude & Appreciation

THANK YOU EUNICE ONITA FOR continuing to be my inspiration reservoir.

Promise

I, _____ PROMISE TO BE MOTIVATED and committed to accomplishing professional greatness on an ongoing basis. I choose not to be hesitant nor reluctant to invest in the suggested resources and to participate in the outlined activities that will help boost my confidence. I will be profoundly bold in my skills, abilities, and career choices. I will recognize and honor that my career choices will usher me to lessons of how to excel in my communication, be efficient in strategies, and be compelling during interactions with other professionals. I am accountable, responsible, and prepared to be in tune with the processes and outcomes that occur during my career journey. I will repeat the affirmations, review the topics, and complete the action list each day. I am proud of my efforts to be confidently motivated to achieve my goals.

Signature _____ Date _____

Contents

Confidently You Bonus Week

Goal Setting: Start with the End in Mind

————

CAREER AFFIRMATION:

I KNOW WHAT I WANT my career outcomes to be. I confidently trust that my career choices are wise and laced with good judgement. My actions intentionally lead me to accomplish my ultimate career goals.

> *"A dream written down with a date becomes a goal. A goal broken down into steps becomes a plan. A plan backed by action makes your dreams come true."*
>
> *~ KAREN CORDAWAY, TEACHER AND WRITER FOR MONEY SAVING ENTHUSIAST*

Your career goals should remain at the top of your mind on an ongoing basis. Be detailed and set your goals to be attainable milestones that complement your career vision. Stretch to develop your skills and abilities to excel in your industry. Celebrate your goal accomplishments once they have been achieved. Share your goals with others to assist you in being accountable and committed. The goals that you identify for yourself should always push you to be your professional best.

Action Item of the Day

Take a moment and reflect on the career goals that you have made in the past. If completed, identify how you did it and why. If you did not fulfill the goal, determine why you did not. Next, applaud your efforts and get excited for a second opportunity to work on improving your goal strategy. Finally, set new completion dates and re-write the goals that you did not fulfill 100 percent or that you need to work on with a new perspective that motivates you.

Action List

List three goals that you have accomplished. Share why the accomplished goals are important to you.

1.

_____

2.

_____

3.

_____

List three goals that you want to revise or repeat. How will revising or repeating the goals help you excel professionally?

1.

_____

2.

_____

3.

_____

Reflections of the day:

Today I accomplished

_____

I learned

_____

I am grateful for

I will invest in

I will repeat

Affirm: I am driven to accomplish my goals today.

Be Accountable to Self

CAREER AFFIRMATION:

I AM ACCOUNTABLE AND HONEST with myself about what I do daily. I am accountable for being my professional and personal best. I do not shy away from my truth nor my actions that I complete (or need to complete) to usher opportunities to me daily.

"Accountability separates the wishers in life from the action-takers that care enough about their future to account for their daily actions."

~ *JOHN DI LEMME, HIGH-END BUSINESS CONSULTANT, STRATEGIC BUSINESS COACH, & AUTHOR*

It is important for you to be accountable to yourself personally and professionally. Choose to be consistent and responsible by responding to the calls of actions that inspire and direct you to follow through. Be accountable to your goals and monitor your success along the way. Life is simply too short not to be responsible for yourself to complete the efforts to fulfill your destiny. Being accountable is one of the best actions that you can take to avoid regrets in different areas of your life.

A – Achieve. Set achievable goals for yourself daily.

C – Conquer. Face your fears and self-doubt head on. Make consistent and dedicated efforts not to let them impact your thought process. Follow-through with being accountable to pursuing your career aspirations.

C – Crave Your Confidence. Be confident in your skills and abilities. Reinforce your faith to being diligent in advancing in your career.

O – Organize. Set aside time daily to organize your computer and physical workplace space.

U – Uplift. Raise your perspective on being accountable to your dreams and legacy. Commit to completing the self-work needed to operate at your professional best.

N – Note Your Actions. Make your outcomes count. You are an example of excellence in the workplace.

T – Triumph. Even when you are at a crossroad of determining your next move for a decision, project, or career move, be firm with yourself to forge ahead and not shrink back or become complacent.

A – Approach. Be actively in tune with the actions you complete to transform your dreams into your reality.

B – Blaze. Be consistent with seeking resources that benefit and advance you as an industry expert or thought leader.

I – Inspire. Keep yourself inspired with verbal affirmations. Remain visually focused on the essential components of your day that keep you on track with your success routines.

L – Launch Logic. Be logically strategic in your daily, weekly, monthly, quarterly, and annual plans. Avoid being random in your planning; make all aspects of your planning connect and flow.

I – Identify. Complete accountability checks to assess how much time it's taking to complete your tasks and the quality of the manner that you're executing them.

T – Tackle Time. Maximize your daily activity by time blocking.

Y – Yell Yes. Say, "yes" to stretching beyond your comfort zone. Be creative and try your ideas.

Action Item of the Day

List three people you can contact to be your accountability partners and be a part of the "Dream Team" that's helping you to
build and execute your dreams. Choose professionals whom you
trust and respect and whose opinions you value. Connect with
professionals who will give you constructive feedback to help
boost you to the next level of your professional best.

Action List

List the outcomes, agreed action items, and specific plans from each conversation with your accountability partners that will assist you in developing your career goals.

Accountability Partner #1.

_____

Accountability Partner #2.

_____

Accountability Partner #3.

_____

Reflections of the day:

Today I accomplished

_____

I learned

_____

I am grateful for

_____

I will invest in

_____

I will repeat

Affirm: I am grateful to have amazing professionals hold me accountable to being my professional best.

Write the Vision

CAREER AFFIRMATION:

I AM A VISIONARY. I write down my goals daily in the past tense as if they are already my reality. I am excited that my career vision is in the process of coming into fruition more and more each day.

"Create a vision that makes you want to
jump out of bed in the morning."

~ *UNKNOWN*

Research and determine what you want to accomplish in your career. Then retreat and construct a paragraph that clearly explains the career success that you intentionally want to experience. Your career vision journaling exercises can be an outline of your career legacy. It'll be a great resource for reviewing and monitoring your career confidence growth over an extended period. It is ideal to journal twice a day—in the morning and during the evening. A useful journaling tip is to write your career vision in a positive tone. Remember that reciting your career vision should not be viewed as a chore but as a time of reiteration of the professional excellence that you were created to accomplish.

Action Item of the Day

Monitor what angers you and makes you envious. Identify ways to minimize the display of negative emotions in your life through journaling, therapy, or spending quality time with your support system. Write your career vision. Log about the professional observations, types of industry knowledge, and profitable outcomes your profession will bring you. Be detailed with your words and desired metrics. Read your career vision on a consistent basis and update quarterly, annually, or as needed.

Action List

Write Your Career Vision.

_____

_____

_____

Are you connected to right opportunities and information that will help develop your career visions? Yes or No?

If no, what steps do you need to complete to be more in sync with executing your career vision?

_____

_____

_____

Reflections of the day:

Today I accomplished

_____

I learned

_____

I am grateful for

_____

I will invest in

_____

I will repeat

_____

Affirm: My career vision is my success compass that inspires me.

Meditation Breeds Productivity

CAREER AFFIRMATION:

I TAKE TIME DAILY TO meditate on the favorable outcomes that my day will generate for me. I am a prosperous professional who focuses on what's important each day to add value and increase productivity to my workplace.

> *"Meditation is a lifelong process. Give it a try. As you get deeper and more disciplined into the process, you'll get deeper and more disciplined in your mind and life."*
>
> ~ BRENDON BURCHARD, AMERICAN AUTHOR ON MOTIVATION, HIGH PERFORMANCE, AND ONLINE MARKETING

E.C. LaMeaux with Gaiam Life, a green lifestyle and yoga brand, shares a 3-step meditation strategy to promote job performance.

Step 1: Design a realistic meditation schedule.
Step 2: Research what type of meditation would be a good fit for you to practice.
Step 3: Expect to see results.

Once you establish a consistent meditation practice, you will begin to view it as a necessity to your daily routine. In addition to the clarity of thoughts, there are multiple health benefits of meditation. If it is a challenge for you to establish a meditation practice on your own, consider retaining a meditation coach or joining a meditation group. Research meditation styles and set a meditation start date.

Journal about your meditation "aha moments" and clarity revelations. During your meditation time, visualize doing what you've journaled and dreamed. If you're not consistent with your meditation practice, remain encouraged and keep up your efforts to become consistent.

Action Item of the Day

Color a mandala. According to Cathy Wong ND, an alternative medicine expert, people who color mandalas can experience a deep sense of calmness and well-being. A mandala is a simple tool that doesn't require any expertise. Coloring a mandala results in combined benefits of art therapy and meditation. Mandalas not only focus your attention, but allow you to express your creative side (which many professionals neglect in their daily lives). Mandala activity books can be found in bookstores and online.

© Career Confident Enterprises LLC

1. You should use colored pencils, crayons, or markers to color your mandala.
2. Color your mandala in a sacred place that is quiet and comfortable for you.
3. Use colors that you gravitate to instinctively. *Don't over-think the colors that you choose to use.*
4. Start to color the mandala.
5. Enjoy the moment.

Action List

List which meditation practices interest you.

1.

_____

2.

_____

3.

_____

How and when are you going to include meditation into your daily success routine?

_____

_____

_____

Reflections of the day:

Today I accomplished

_____

I learned

_____

I am grateful for

_____

I will invest in

_____

I will repeat

_____

Affirm: I view my meditation practice as time well spent.

Affirm Your Success

CAREER AFFIRMATION:

I CONFIDENTLY DECLARE MY CAREER success daily. I speak positively about my abilities and skills. I am continually mindful that my words frame my day. I am a success story. I accomplish great things on a continual basis.

> *"Your mind is a powerful thing. When you fill it with positive thoughts, your life will start to change."*

> ~ *UNKNOWN*

Surround yourself with words that inspire you to be your best. Utilize your everyday tools and visuals with words that represent your goals and dreams. Promote uplifting affirmations through your screen savers, home décor, jewelry, journals, etc. Speak with excitement, enthusiasm, and repeat your affirmations in the present tense as if it is already your reality.

Activity of the Day

Write a list of 10 words that inspire you to accomplish greatness. Get the creative juices flowing and post your affirmations in places for you to see and say them at least two times daily.

Suggestions: Create an affirmation board only with words, wear affirmation jewelry, or set phone reminders that prompt you to say empowering declarations.

Action List

Now that you've identified the words that inspired you, write down why you chose those words and how they empower you to be your professional best.

_____

_____

_____

_____

_____

Reflections of the day:

Today I accomplished

_____

I learned

_____

I am grateful for

_____

I will invest in

_____

I will repeat

_____

Affirm: I choose my words wisely.

Welcome Support

CAREER AFFIRMATION:

I AM THANKFUL FOR MY support system that is full of genuine people from my personal and professional circles and are authentic cheerleaders of my success.

"Evaluate the people in your life; then promote,
demote, or terminate. You're the CEO of your life."

~ UNKNOWN

Support System. n. a network of people who provide an individual with practical or emotional support. *Academic Medical Dictionary*

Your support system should be a group of people who you trust to hold you accountable to being your best self and push you to move past your perceived limits. Your support system can be made up of family, friends, mentors, experts, and professional peers who you view as trusted personal cheerleaders. You want to surround yourself with goal-getters who confidently celebrate others. When communicating with members of your support system, you and your partners should feel empowered and have a refreshed perspective to remain focused on accomplishing greatness. Your support system should commit to not complaining and consistently focus on sharing experiences in a positive manner that produce solutions.

Action Item of the Day

Today spend time reviewing the quality over the quantity of your support system. Who do you learn from consistently? Who encourages you? Who holds you accountable for producing your best at all times? Who adds value to your life?

Action List

What is your definition of a support system?

_____

_____

How does your support system inspire you to accomplish greatness?

_____

Reflections of the day:

Today I accomplished

_____

I learned

_____

I am grateful for

_____

I will invest in

_____

I will repeat

_____

Affirm: I am grateful that my support system empowers me to be my professional best.

Focus on Priorities

———

Career Affirmation:

I CAN SUCCESSFULLY FOCUS ON my tasks and priorities that contribute to being successful in the workplace daily.

"Focus on being productive instead of busy."

~ Unknown

May Busch of May Busch & Associates consulting practice in the UK suggests that it is important for professionals to focus on three priorities at a time. According to Busch, three goals are easy to focus on and complete. These objectives can be a revolving point of discussion or itemized on a task list. Be sure to have a crystal clear understanding of what is important to your being successful in your workplace. Sometimes new and seasoned professionals can intentionally or unintentionally get caught up on focus points that are not in line with components of their daily, weekly, monthly, quarterly, or annual metric expectations. Focus on what matters to your success and avoid being involved in interactions or conversations that deter you from being fully present and focused.

Action Item of the Day

Today confirm that you have a clear understanding of your company's culture—a culture that you are a part of creating. Take the time to complete an analysis of the tasks and guidelines that you focused on in the past and what target points you may need to keep or replace to be productive in your workplace. Determine which areas (related to the company's culture) need more focus and develop an action plan to address it.

Action List

What is your interpretation of your employer's culture?

Wins:

Areas of improvement and action plan:

Rate your daily productivity:

Above Average   Average   Below Average

How can you be more focused in the workplace?

Reflections of the day:

Today I accomplished

I learned

I am grateful for

I will invest in

_____

I will repeat

_____

Affirm: My ability to master prioritizing connects me to fulfilling my destiny.

Be Flexible and Sharp

CAREER AFFIRMATION:

I DO NOT PLACE ANY limits on myself and what I can accomplish professionally. I take the time to acknowledge and understand that my career path can change. The key is keeping my skills sharp, maintaining a great attitude, and being on the lookout for fantastic opportunities.

"Dear destiny, I am ready now."

~ UNKNOWN

Planning to advance beyond your current role is a part of career pathing. One thing to keep in mind while career planning is that career change is inevitable. It is fundamental and essential to keep your skills sharp, keep a great attitude, and be open to new opportunities. While in preparation for your next career opportunity, you must know that there is great reward for not complaining as you improve your people and industry skills. Today I encourage you to remain encouraged with the truth that *what is for you is for you.* Affirm within yourself that you have not been denied your career aspirations. The right opportunity is en route to you. Be ready with confidence!

Action Item of the Day

Create a traditional or electronic vision board via Pinterest or a presentation software. Collect your favorite magazines, quotes, and pictures and start cutting out the words and images that you connect with being successful. Use an adhesive to stick them to a cardboard poster. Display the vision board in a location where you can easily see it daily.

Action List

What lessons have you learned from your career detours and advancements? How have they made you a better professional?

_____

_____

_____

What is the next career goal that you're working to accomplish for yourself?

_____

_____

_____

Reflections of the day:

Today I accomplished

_____

I learned

_____

I am grateful for

_____

I will invest in

_____

I will repeat

_____

Affirm: I believe that I am able and prepared to navigate my career path.

DAY 9

Create Multiple Income Streams

CAREER AFFIRMATION:

I AM CREATIVE, AND I attract money through multiple streams of income.

> *"Successful people make money. It's not that
> people who make money become successful,
> but that successful people attract money.
> They bring success to what they do."*
>
> ~ WAYNE DYER, AMERICAN PHILOSOPHER,
> AUTHOR, & MOTIVATIONAL SPEAKER

Diversify your work with more than one stream of income through freelance opportunities and investments. Depending on one job to maintain your lifestyle and secure the financial stability of your future can potentially be challenging with the rise of the freelance economy. The freelance community is comprised of independent contractors, moonlighters, diversified workers, temporary workers, and business owners. Having multiple income streams is also a stress reliever knowing that you are not reliant on one avenue. Retreat and get your creative juices flowing. Create passive income for yourself or launch an online business. Determine how you can make money from what interests you and know what business platform you'll have to commit to in order to generate a profitable return.

Action Item of the Day

It's time to make your passion your paycheck. Spend time discovering what your multiple streams of income will be.

1. What services and products interest you?

2. Identify which business platforms interest you.

3. Which products, services, and business platforms do you feel you can commit to and want to continue to learn?

4. Who can mentor you through this process?

5. What will your start-up and projected monthly expenses be?

6. Who are your competitors?

Action List

List income streams that can generate a solid return on your investment of time and resources.

1.
2.
3.
4.
5.
6.
7.

What is the next income stream that you're going to research and launch?

Reflections of the day:

Today I accomplished

I learned

I am grateful for

I will invest in

I will repeat

Affirm: I am an idea generator who confidently creates multiple streams of income.

DAY 10

Celebrate Others

———

CAREER AFFIRMATION:

I CONFIDENTLY SUPPORT THE ACCOMPLISHMENTS of others and positively interact with others while networking with leaders, mentors, and peers.

> *"Celebrate the success of others as you*
> *would want others to celebrate yours.*
> *What goes around comes around."*

~ *ANONYMOUS*

Take time to show up and celebrate others' accomplishments and events. Confidently celebrating others is not only fun but a possible opportunity to network and work with other amazing professionals. Your ability to celebrate someone else is a reflection of the career confidence that reigns within you. Giving good cheer boosts trust in the capacity to work well with others and be successful in collaborative projects.

Action Item of the Day

Send a kudos note or email to a peer who is doing awesome things in the workplace and industry. Post a congratulatory message on a social media platform acknowledging the success of a peer.

Show up to an event that a peer or an industry influencer is hosting and plan to promote and/or invest in their products or services. Choose to be the example of how to encourage others to be their professional best.

Action List

Which professionals do you plan to celebrate? Why?
1.
_____

2.
_____

3.
_____

How do you plan to celebrate those professionals?
1.
_____

2.
_____

3.
_____

Reflections of the day:

Today I accomplished
_____

I learned
_____

I am grateful for
_____

I will invest in

_____

I will repeat

_____

Affirm: Celebrating the accomplishments of others is an act of confidence.

Be Healthy

CAREER AFFIRMATION:

I MAKE HEALTHY CHOICES. I am worthy of my own time and efforts to properly nourish myself daily through exercise, meditation, and proper food intake. I take good care of mind, body, and spirit.

"The first wealth is health."

~ RALPH WALDO EMERSON, AMERICAN
ESSAYIST, LECTURER, & POET

Suggested Healthy Actions:

1. Eat healthy daily.
2. Exercise and stretch your body regularly.
3. Be patient with yourself.
4. Rest daily.
5. Reflect for clarity and peace of mind.
6. Laugh often.
7. Stay hydrated with water and juices.
8. Detox from social media periodically.
9. Don't take yourself seriously all the time.
10. Accept help from others professionally and personally.

Action Item of the Day

What you choose to eat can impact the direction of your mood and attitude. Assess your snack choices and intake in between meals. Determine if you need to revise or improve your weekly exercise schedule or routine. Create a meal plan for yourself that you can commit to and have a selection of creative edible choices when preparing.

Action List

What are your healthy best practices?

_____

_____

_____

What are a few healthy activities that you're interested in trying?

_____

_____

_____

Reflections of the day:

Today I accomplished

_____

I learned

_____

I am grateful for

_____

I will invest in

_____

I will repeat

_____

Affirm: I am an example of good health.

Know Your Worth

CAREER AFFIRMATION:

I AM DILIGENT IN MY efforts to acquire the necessary experience, expertise, and professional network. I position myself to receive my desired financial worth in exchange for my skills and services.

> *"Know your worth. Know the difference between what you're getting and what you deserve."*

> *~ UNKNOWN*

Assess your skills and contributions on a quarterly or annual basis. Be prepared to negotiate and position yourself for next level career opportunities. Be confident in your abilities and gain the required experiences and expertise while in transition. Every professional's journey to career advancement is distinctively different. You will not always have to start from scratch in your career to demonstrate your worth to an employer. You may experience the combination of all your professional experiences and lessons transitioning you to the right role and pay level at precisely the right time. The key to knowing your worth is to not shrink back or be reluctant in nominating yourself to participate in activities and responsibilities that interest you and add value to your professional repertoire.

Action Item of the Day

Review your job description or business plan and assess if you're earning your worth based on your contribution to the role. Research salary range and advancement potential for your role. Prepare to negotiate your salary and responsibilities as needed. Develop a clear understanding of your career growth and development plan. Know your competitors, their product, and historical operational data to assist in comparing and determining financial benchmarks and course of action to accomplish your financial goals.

Action List

What is the pay range for your skills, knowledge, and abilities in the current role and industry that you work?

_____

_____

_____

If you perceive that you need to gain experience to be paid your worth. How can you acquire that experience? For example, change of job, second job, volunteering, more time in your current role, willingness to move, etc.

_____

_____

_____

Reflections of the day:

Today I accomplished

_____

I learned

_____

I am grateful for

_____

I will invest in

_____

I will repeat

_____

Affirm: I prepare and position myself to get paid my worth professionally.

Invest In Yourself

CAREER AFFIRMATION:

I CONNECT TO RESOURCES THAT will help shift and propel me to a higher level in my career. I am confident in the truth that I am a worthy investment.

> *"If you want to be truly successful, invest in yourself to get the knowledge you need to find your unique factor. When you find it and focus on it and persevere your success will blossom."*

> ~ SIDNEY MADWED, LYRICIST & AUTHOR

One quality of a confident professional is in their willingness to always be a student. It is important to complete a self-analysis about your skills and abilities. Determine in which areas you excel and which areas you need to improve. You may need help getting the trailblazer in you to confidently shine brightly and be seen as the credible resource that you are. Don't hesitate to determine if you need to invest in different classes or hire a coach who will help you advance as a subject-matter expert in your industry. Also, commit to participating in leadership development programs on an ongoing basis by attending seminars, workshops, or retreats. Attend different sessions virtually and in-person to determine which format is the right fit for you.

Action Item of the Day

Invest in the book, *Strength Finder 2.0* by Tom Rath. This book will help you identify your strengths and learn to utilize them to perform at your best. The suggested time to read the book is before or after quarterly and/or annual reviews. This is an excellent book to use individually or in a team-centric business setting.

Complete the crossword puzzle. It also suggests areas that you can invest your time developing to excel professionally.

Workplace Skills & Abilities

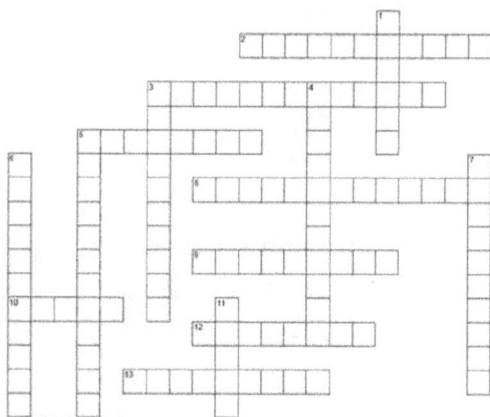

© 2018 Career Coalition Enterprises LLC

ACROSS

2 Willingness to change or compromise in different circumstances
3 Skills and abilities that cause the exchange of information
5 The process of making plans for an organization or event
8 A thinker who focuses on the problem as stated and strategizes to achieve a solution
9 Detailed coordination of business operations involving many people, facilities, or supplies
10 Conduct an official examination of business processes or financials
12 The ability to accept results and delayed circumstances without getting angry or upset
13 The act of completing market research and advertising plan to promote or sell a product

DOWN

1 Thought out the judgement of when something should take place
3 Engaged in the business of giving expert advice to people working in a professional or technical field
4 The process of working together with professionals to the same end
5 A productive effort that can be a measured by an outcome
6 Conversations to reach an agreement or compromise
7 The ability to be imaginative in generating ideas
11 The action of selling goods and services

Action List

What classes are you interested in taking for your personal and professional growth?

_____

_____

_____

Reflections of the day:

Today I accomplished

_____

I learned

_____

I am grateful for

_____

I will invest in

_____

I will repeat

_____

Affirm: I am a worthy investment.

Polish Your Look

CAREER AFFIRMATION:

I CARRY MYSELF CONFIDENTLY AND dress how I want to be addressed socially and professionally. I am a worthy investment of my resources that help me present a polished, positive, and note-worthy career image.

"Style is a way to say who you are without having to speak."

~ RACHEL ZOE, AMERICAN FASHION DESIGNER

Your overall career image is an unspoken resumé. Be confident in the way that you present yourself through your daily attire and your office space décor. Dress appropriately for your professional industry. Take notice of the clothing style leadership follows and what the dress code expectations are for your role. If applicable, then determine how you can add your personal flare that portrays you confidently at your best.

Next, what does your office space say about you? Complete an analysis of your professional surroundings. What does your desk space reflect about you? Does it project your ideal career image in any form? No matter the dynamics of your office space, take the time to make it personal.

Action Item of the Day

Visit your favorite home and office décor retailer. Pick up affirmation signage or frames to display pictures that motivate you and make you smile. Invest in a personal shopper or stylist to help upgrade your wardrobe (styling services can be completed in-person or virtually). Know which colors look best on you and which ones inspire you.

Action List

What will you do today to polish your office look?

_____

_____

_____

What updates do you need to make to your career wardrobe?

_____

_____

_____

Reflections of the day:

Today I accomplished

_____

I learned

_____

I am grateful for

_____

I will invest in

_____

I will repeat

_____

Affirm: My career image is polished and professional.

DAY 15

Decode Your Body Language

———

CAREER AFFIRMATION:
MY BODY LANGUAGE REITERATES MY self-esteem and voice. I am confident in all forms of communication.

"Your body communicates as well as your
mouth. Don't contradict yourself."

~ ALLEN RUDDOCK, UNITED KINGDOM PROJECT
& PROGRAM MANAGEMENT CONSULTANT

Your body language speaks volumes. It displays your voice, attitude, and confidence level before any words flow from your lips. Non-verbal cues can even determine the authenticity and truth of a message. Research appropriate body languages to use in professional settings including group situations, presentations, and meetings, and be aware of what you're actually saying.

Action Item of the Day

Pay attention to your body language throughout the day. Take notice of your handshake, eye contact, and the way that you interact with colleagues during meetings and conversations. Observe the body language of other professionals throughout the day as well.

Action List

What is your body language like when your mood or attitude changes? What does it convey when you're happy, frustrated, upset, or feeling successful?

_____

_____

_____

What are a few gestures that you can do more or less of to improve your body language?

_____

_____

_____

Reflections of the day:

Today I accomplished

_____

I learned

_____

I am grateful for

_____

I will invest in

_____

I will repeat

_____

Affirm: I am self-assured and carry myself in an approachable manner.

Read. Read. Read.

————

CAREER AFFIRMATION:

I AM AN AVID READER or listener of books that add value to my knowledge base. I am consistently learning to expand my perspective, explore new options, complete tasks, and dream bigger.

> *"Only you can increase your value by reading*
> *and gaining knowledge. Do you want to*
> *increase your income level? You must increase*
> *your value; you must read more!"*
>
> ~ STACIA PIERCE, AUTHOR, SUCCESS
> COACH, AND ENTREPRENEUR

The benefits of reading go beyond self-improvement and improving your vocabulary. Reading takes you on adventures while improving your concentration and has the ability to boost your career confidence. Taking the time to become more informed, proficient, and credible as an industry expert is valuable. Choosing to be a knowledgeable professional permits you to become a sought-after resource among professional peers in your workplace and industry.

No matter your reading platform preference, it is important to read and commit to staying in-the-know of what is going on in your industry, community, and global affairs. Books are also tools that many professionals use to achieve resolution in a workplace. By reading selective books with colleagues, you can gain experience from other professionals. You can help bridge communication, generate ideas, and build a cohesive and productive team.

Action Item of the Day

Commit to reading or listening to at least one audio book per month. Visit your local book store. Check out the top promoted books by the store and spend time canvassing the magazine stand. Challenge yourself to read one industry magazine a week. Become familiar with what's going on in the news—locally and globally. Learn the names of the magazines that share content for a particular niche that interests you. Find a new recipe to try, or find out the current trends in fashion, home, and entertainment.

Write a list of three books that you *need* and *want* to read for pleasure that will help you advance in your career. Here are a few suggested classic reads:

* *How to Win Friends & Influence People* by Dale Carnegie
* *The 7 Habits of Highly Effective People* by Stephen R. Covey
* *The Power of Positive Thinking* by Norman Vincent Peale

For Leisure:
1. _____
2. _____
3. _____

For Career:
1. _____
2. _____
3. _____

Action List

List three goals that you have accomplished. Write why the accomplished goals are important to you.

1.
_____

2.
_____

3.
_____

List three goals that you want to revise or repeat. Write about how revising or repeating the goals will help you excel professionally.

1.
_____

2.
_____

3.
_____

Reflections of the day:

Today I will accomplish
_____

Career reflection of the day:

I learned
_____

I am grateful for

_____

I will invest in

_____

I will repeat

_____

Affirm: I am driven to accomplish my goals today.

DAY 17

Be a Grammar Slammer

CAREER AFFIRMATION:

I WRITE WELL AND COMMUNICATE effectively with professionals in different business settings.

*"Good grammar should be the norm
and not the exception."*

~ MICHELE BADIE, CAREER CONFIDENCE
COACH, BLOGGER, & PODCASTER

The foundation of effective communication is good grammar. Participating in result-oriented conversations warrants engaging, powerful, and proper usage of words in business settings. Take time to use proper grammar in all of your professional communication. Good grammar reflects your level of professional competency. Choose to shine brightly in your workplace because you speak and write well.

Suggested Grammar Resources:

- Grammarly.com
- *The Elements of Style, Fourth Edition* by William Strunk Jr. and E.B. White
- Download The Free Dictionary app by Farlex, Inc.
- Listen to Grammar Girl Quick and Dirty Tips for Better Writing podcast.

Action Item of the Day

- Enrich your vocabulary and learn a new word a day. Use the word at least once a day.
- Commit to not using text language in any form during professional communication.
- Pay attention to the words you use in different professional conversations. Are you using the words in the correct tense?

Action List

What can you do today to improve your writing?

_____

_____

_____

Reflections of the day:

Today I accomplished

_____

Career reflection of the day:

I learned

_____

I am grateful

_____

I will invest in

_____

I will repeat

_____

Affirm: I write and use proper grammar well.

Active Listening is a Game Changer

———

CAREER AFFIRMATION:
I AM AN ACTIVE LISTENER. I listen to understand.

> *"One of the most sincere forms of respect is
> actually listening to what another has to say."*

> ~ *BRYANT H. MCGILL, AUTHOR*

Become an active listener. Make it a point to be respectful and not get caught up in distractions nor formulate your response during your conversation when you should be listening to the speaker. Be cognitive that your body language is in sync with showing that you're actively listening. Keep good eye contact and engage in the conversation. Wait to give your opinion until after the speaker has shared all of their points. Re-confirm what the speaker said and respond appropriately with a suggested resolution, if applicable. Aim to maintain a positive tone during the communication.

Action Item of the Day

Read the book, *Power Listening* by Bernard T. Ferrari. Many leaders and corporate executives read this book annually as a reminder of the importance of active listening and why it should be practiced daily. Attempt to not get distracted by conversations and other communications or social media platforms. Be present in conversations— in person and on the phone.

Action List

In what business settings are you going to focus on being a better active listener?

_____

_____

_____

What adjustments can you make with your body language to demonstrate that you're an active listener?

_____

_____

_____

Reflections of the day:

Today I accomplished

_____

I learned

_____

I am grateful for

_____

I will invest in

_____

I will repeat

_____

Affirm: I pick up good business and success tips and clues when I take time to listen to others.

Boot the Imposter Syndrome

―――――

CAREER AFFIRMATION:

I AM CONFIDENT. I CHOOSE to ignore thoughts of self-doubt and confidently affirm that I am in the right place at the right time to receive the lesson, resource, or promotion that I need to advance in my career.

> *"It's not who you are that holds you back.*
> *It's who you think you're not."*
>
> *~ UNKNOWN*

Caltech Counseling Center defines the imposter syndrome as a collection of feelings of inadequacy that persists even in the face of information that indicates that the opposite is true. It is experienced internally as chronic self-doubt and feelings of intellectual fraudulence. Caroline Ghosn, CEO and co-founder of Love League—a social network dedicated to elevating the career of Gen Y professionals—suggests four ways to reclaim your career confidence and ignore the "imposter syndrome" that can fuel self-doubt.

1. Embrace moments of doubt.
2. See beyond the setback.
3. Find a mentor.
4. Never aim for perfection.

We all at some point have questioned an outcome or action that can ignite self-doubt within us. One may wonder whether or not their skills and qualifications are up to par for a certain career opportunity. It is critically important to demonstrate courage and confidence and dismiss the whispers of the imposter syndrome. Shift your focus to your lessons from your acquired experience and the professional accomplishments that you've made. Verbally affirm to yourself that you're worthy of the opportunity and continue to prepare to be successful in the role.

Action Item of the Day

Write a list of your professional achievements and post them in a place where you can see them daily. Let your results serve as a source of inspiration. Review the list frequently. Viewing your impressive outcomes (measurable and non-measurable) will help you silence thoughts of self-doubt.

Action List

List your professional achievements.
1.
_____
2.
_____
3.
_____
4.
_____
5.
_____
6.
_____

Reflections of the day:

Today I accomplished
_____

I learned
_____

I am grateful for

_____

I will invest in

_____

Affirm: I don't respond to the whispers of doubt.

The Option of Remote

CAREER AFFIRMATION:

I GIVE MYSELF PERMISSION TO pursue the career freedom that I desire with courage and determination.

> *"Choose a job you love, and you will never*
> *have to work a day in your life."*
>
> ~ CONFUCIUS, CHINESE TEACHER, EDITOR,
> POLITICIAN, AND PHILOSOPHER

A brick and mortar work environment is not for every professional. Maybe you're a professional road warrior who is ready for a career change. You want to work remotely or in a co-work space that allows you to travel the globe? The evolution of the freelance community has created many opportunities. In 2014, Sara Horowitz, Founder and Executive Director of Freelancers Union, and Fabio Rosati, CEO of Elance-oDesk, shared landmark survey results through the Freelancers Union indicating that more than 53 million Americans–34 percent of the U.S. workforce— are working as freelancers. The study defined freelancers as "individuals who have engaged in supplemental, temporary, or project-or-contract-based work in the past 12 months."

There are many freelance opportunities in technology such as project management, creative, internet, and marketing. It's time to take the walls off your career path and navigate your way to the career experience that you desire. Be patient with the process but remain diligent in your efforts.

Action Item of the Day

Read *The 4-Hour Workweek* by Timothy Ferris. This book is a great resource on how to successfully transition to working remotely part-time or full-time as a contractor or as an entrepreneur. Also, subscribe to The Tim Ferris Show podcast. This general business podcast is a medley of different professional game-changers and trailblazers sharing their lessons, resources, and personal knowledge of what has made them successful in work and life.

Action List

Is freelance or remote work a right fit for you? Why or why not?

_____

_____

_____

Research and identify the freelance and remote work opportunities in your industries.

_____

_____

_____

Reflections of the day:

Today I accomplished

_____

I learned

_____

I am grateful for

_____

I will invest in

_____

I will repeat

_____

Affirm: I am open to learning more and pursing different free-lance and remote career opportunities.

Conflict Delivers Opportunities

CAREER AFFIRMATION:

I COMMUNICATE WITH MY COLLEAGUES with an open mind. I am a resolution generator. I quickly identify opportunities presented in a conflict which refreshes mindsets, creates new ideas, and upgrades processes.

"In the middle of difficulty lies opportunity."

~ ALBERT EINSTEIN, THEORETICAL PHYSICIST

Choose to be fully present with open ears and ask non-emotional yet valid questions in the midst of conflict resolution. Be courageous and directly address the conflict. Stick to the facts and the relevant points to determine and attempt to understand the perspective of each person involved. Actively listen and be alert to any opportunities that are awaiting in the midst of the difference of opinions. Aim to have a win-win outcome.

Action Item of the Day

Conflict is like navigating a maze. We explore different paths to find our way to the goal. Each path has different turns and sometimes requires us to re-route our efforts and perspective. Along the way, we improve our ability to strategize, be patient, and focus on getting to the result. Complete the maze.

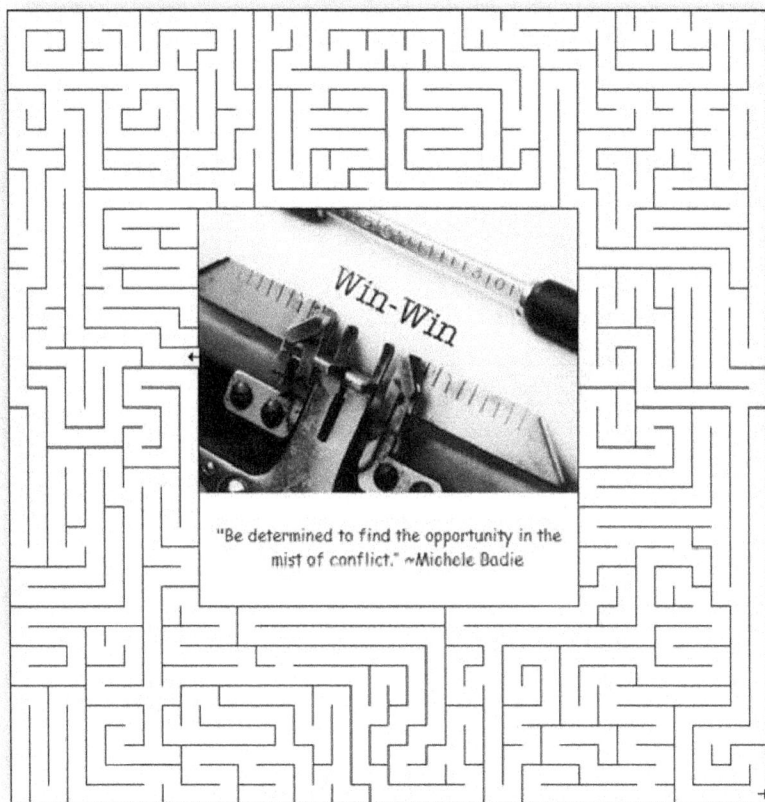

"Be determined to find the opportunity in the mist of conflict." ~Michele Badie

© Career Confident Enterprises LLC

Action List

What is your conflict resolution strategy in the workplace?

_____

_____

_____

Would not avoiding conflict help you or hinder you with your people skills?

_____

_____

Reflections of the day:

Today I will accomplish

_____

I learned

_____

I am grateful for

_____

I will invest in

_____

I will repeat

_____

Affirm: I become a better communicator from the lessons that I learn from conflict.

Confidently You
Bonus Week

———

Be In the Know

CAREER AFFIRMATION:

I AM A SUBJECT-MATTER EXPERT who confidently shares current and relevant industry knowledge that provides solutions and propels businesses.

"Always desire to learn something useful."

~ SOPHOCLES, ANCIENT GREEK TRAGEDIAN

Study your industry. Regardless of where you are to being a subject-matter expert (SME) in your career, it is always important to be in position to upgrade your knowledge and remain "in the know" of what's going on in your industry. Be ravenous about expanding your knowledge bandwidth in understanding the past, present, and future of what cultivated your industry to be what it is today. Sign up for industry newsletters and follow other subject-matter experts on their social media channels. Confidently share quality content of other influencers and respected peers.

Action Item of the Day

Time to test your industry knowledge.

1. Who are the top thought leaders in your industry?
2. Do you speak and understand your industry's language?
3. Are you able to efficiently use the software programs associated with your industry?
4. What are the top periodicals in your industry? Do you read them? Why or why not?
5. What are the past, present, and future trends in your industry?
6. What certifications are required in your industry? Do you need them? Why or why not?

Action List

Being a subject-matter expert at any given position within an industry is valuable.

How would you rate yourself as a subject-matter expert?

Above average   Average   Below Average

What can you do to be more confident in your knowledge, skills, and abilities to be a subject-matter expert?

_____

_____

_____

Reflections of the day:

Today I will accomplish

_____

Career reflection of the day:

I learned

_____

I am grateful for

_____

I will invest in

_____

I will repeat

_____

Affirm: I research and understand the trends and data of my industry.

Be Organized

CAREER AFFIRMATION:

I AM ORGANIZED IN HOW I complete tasks and maintain my personal and professional space. I am willing to stay orderly to make regular room for good things and opportunities to find me. I take action every day to prepare for my next level of professional greatness.

> *"No business can succeed in any great degree*
> *without being properly organized."*
>
> ~ *JAMES CASH PENNEY, AMERICAN*
> *BUSINESSMAN AND ENTREPRENEUR*

Below are some benefits of being organized:

* Increased productivity
* More efficient with time
* Reduces clutter in your workplace
* Presents a polished business image
* Ease to prioritize tasks

Action Item of the Day

Read *The Life-Changing Magic of Tidying Up* by Marie Kondo and develop a new understanding about the benefits of being organized. Create a system of how you're going to keep your workspace and home organized. Get creative. Incorporate feng shui ideas and invest in organizational tools that are visually appealing to you.

Action List

How do you stay organized during the day?

_____

_____

_____

Do you feel being organized throughout your work day is important? Why or Why not?

_____

What focus area are you going to make a strong effort to be more organized starting today?

_____

Reflections of the day:

Today I accomplished

_____

Career reflection of the day:

I learned

_____

I am grateful for

_____

I will invest in

_____

I will repeat

_____

Affirm: Being organized helps me to have clarity in my thoughts and use my time wisely.

Be Curious

CAREER AFFIRMATION:

I AM INTRIGUED BY MY personal surroundings and professional environment. I want to learn more good things about my industry and its leaders. My curiosity makes me a witty professional. I can dream bigger and have a defined focus on the important factors that contribute to my success.

> *"Be curious always! For knowledge will not acquire you; you must acquire it."*
>
> ~ SUDIE E. BACK, PH. D., ADDICTION SERVICES PROFESSOR & AUTHOR

You're a genius. You are capable of being an inventor, a thought leader, an educator—the list goes on. Having a curious mind keeps you in a learning mode and keeps your learning perspective fresh. It becomes your flashlight for helping you navigate your way to making your profound professional mark in your industry.

Action Item of the Day

Be adventurous. Push your curiosity limits by changing your everyday environment. Have fun planning and taking a trip to a different country. Shop at a new store. Watch a movie or attend a concert that you wouldn't normally choose. Be fully present at the moment and connect with the lesson or memory you receive from your curiosity.

Action List

What topics are you curious to learn more about today?

_____

_____

_____

How has your curiosity been beneficial to your career?

_____

_____

_____

Reflections of the day:

Today I accomplished

_____

I learned

_____

I am grateful for

_____

I will invest in

_____

I will repeat

_____

Affirm: My curiosity introduces me to new skills and perspectives.

Success Routines

———

CAREER AFFIRMATION:

I AM FAITHFUL IN DEVELOPING my success habits on a continual basis. I am a success magnet, and the habits that I perform daily will make me more effective, efficient, and prosperous.

"We are what we repeatedly do. Excellence,
then, is not an act, but a habit."

~ UNKNOWN

It is important for you to remain on the success attraction path by committing to executing the tasks that keep you focused on your goals, items needed to be accomplished on your to-do lists, and new ideas that will propel you in your career. Ask yourself, "How consistent am I with my daily success habits?" Then ponder,

"Am I affirming my day?"

"Who are the goal-getters that I'm chatting with throughout my day?"

"Am I starting my day early and being consistent with my efforts to breed success in my life?"

"Am I making healthy choices about my mental and physical health?"

Repetition is key to establishing a solid foundation of success habits. Here are some success habit suggestions:

1. Start your day an hour earlier.
2. Affirm your day.
3. Read informative data and motivational resources.
4. Be mindful of what you listen to (music, audio, or people of influence).
5. Eat breakfast, eat well.
6. Write a "To-Do" list.
7. Be grateful.
8. Exercise.
9. Be organized.
10. Develop a strong work ethic.

Action Item of the Day

Success routines take time to develop. Be observant of your current habits and determine what changes you can make. Search for focus areas that can apply to you in the word search below. Then determine which ones you're going to make essential components to your success routines.

Find the words in the grid. Words can go horizontally, vertically and diagonally in all eight directions.

```
M Y N Y N O I T C E L F E R F P Z Y C
N R Y H T L A E H V P T A E P E R D P
C N X Z X C O N S I S T E N T T N W Q
E R H G C N P T R T H K C Z H A B I T
I N D S K N L P N C C R F O C U S E D
J N I R L U T M Z A J X T C V X L R M
F G V L S A Y C M O G X O F P D Y F B
L M R E P L O R E R M U N S R B S A Y
Q E R E S I L G Y P N P E M P Y E F T
E D J J X T C L Q T X N T Y N C H F I
C I M O W C Q S A K I E V E N Q J I S
N T X B U T E B I T T I R E L R N R O
E A K H V R L L U D S G I N F S V M I
D T B V D E N O L U Y R P L L S K A R
I I L Y G Y R A A E E C B D T E Q T U
F O B Y W M L L L P N R H A Z C F I C
N N M P T D I D X I N C K I Q C X O T
O M V L X Z V E M K N N E L C U M N T
C R N P E K P T J M B G T Y R S Q Z M
```

ACCOUNTABLE	EXPECT	MEDITATION
AFFIRMATION	EXPERIENCE	PROACTIVE
CONFIDENCE	FOCUSED	REFLECTION
CONSISTENT	GOALS	REPEAT
CURIOSITY	HABIT	RESULTS
DAILY	HEALTHY	ROUTINES
DISCIPLINE	INVEST	SUCCESS
EXCELLENCE	JOURNALING	SYNERGY

Action List

Which success routines are you going to adopt into your daily, weekly, or monthly routine?

1.

_____

2.

_____

3.

_____

Reflections of the day:

Today I will accomplished

_____

I learned

_____

I am grateful for

_____

I will invest in

_____

I will repeat

_____

Affirm: I am dedicated to repeating my success routines on an ongoing basis.

Fast Action Alert

———

CAREER AFFIRMATION:

I AM AN EXAMPLE OF excellence. I confidently take quick action in pursuing my career goals with a fearless mindset.

"Action conquers fear."

~ PETER NIVIO ZARLENGA, AUTHOR

Many exciting ideas develop in our thoughts daily. We were born to create; therefore, it is important for us not to delay in writing down ideas or to brainstorm with a colleague. Be confident in your ideas by creating and developing plans to transition the ideas from thought to reality. Choose a personal theme song that will motivate you in good cheer to have a fast action perspective.

Schedule time to meditate at least 15 minutes on one of the questions below that can assist in sparking a quick call to action with your career goals of any size or level. Be honest with yourself and accountable for your goals.

1. What immediate action can I take today to complete a challenging task?
2. Identify one thing in your career that's been complacent and think about how you're going to course correct that particular topic.
3. What thoughts of fear, doubt, or negative experiences are interfering with your taking fast action with things relevant to your career?

Based on your answers, set a plan that has different levels of fast action outcomes. Identify the need, develop a plan, and determine the follow-up actions that you can complete daily.

Action Item of the Day

Today, if applicable, course correct how you choose to respond to ideas and opportunities that will advance you in your career. The shift in your actions may be small but significantly impactful to your productivity. Taking action is a personal process that will help determine how you will address different professional scenarios that present themselves.

Identify a need: Become certified in a certain skill.

Develop a plan: Research class offerings, cost, required time, and credentials needed.

Follow-up action:

> Monday- Research class offerings and availability.
> Tuesday - Identify top three class offerings.
> Wednesday - Contact and request information, including cost.
> Thursday - Review schedule and determine when you can register for the first class.
> Friday - Complete application and register, or plan a budget and determine when you can register and pay for the class according to its availability.

Action List

What's your personal theme song?

_____

_____

_____

List three tasks that can be accomplished to create a fast action plan.

1. _____

2. _____

3. _____

Create an action list for one of the tasks.

Monday: _____

Tuesday: _____

Wednesday: _____

Thursday: _____

Friday: _____

Reflections of the day:

Today I accomplished

_____

I learned

_____

I am grateful for

_____

I will invest in

_____

I will repeat

_____

Affirm: I have fantastic outcomes because I take fast action.

Be Happy

CAREER AFFIRMATION:

I DECLARE THAT PEACE OF mind is mine. I choose to connect to something or someone who makes me happy daily.

"Whoever is happy will make others happy too."

~ UNKNOWN

Connect to the insightful content in *Before Happiness* and *The Happiness Advantage* by New York Times Bestselling author Shawn Achor. He promotes that your happiness has a direct connection to being confident. The duration of time and how we choose to process our reactions, perspective, and words are all connected to being happy and confident. It is a great reflection point to revert to as a daily motivator. Shawn shared an ancient Greek quote about the definition of happiness. *"[Happiness] is the joy you feel striving toward your potential."* Applicable to the opinion that if professionals choose, they can connect continuously to being confidently happy and at peace with their career choices and journeys.

Action Item of the Day

Choose not to dwell on experiences or thoughts that have impacted you negatively. Focus on a person, place, or thing that makes you smile. Plan a staycation or vacation. Send a note of thanks to someone within your personal and professional life who you've shared and created happy memories with. Take a long walk and reflect on your success, valued lessons, and the joy points throughout your career and life.

Action List

What is your definition of happy?

_____

_____

_____

What are a few activities that makes you happy?
1. _____
2. _____
3. _____

Reflections of the day:

Today I accomplished

_____

I learned

_____

I am grateful for

_____

I will invest in

_____

I will repeat

_____

Affirm: I choose to define what makes me happy personally and professionally.

Stretch Often

CAREER AFFIRMATION:
I AM WILLING TO TRY something new today.

> *"Try to keep your mind open to possibilities and*
> *your mouth closed on matters that you don't know*
> *about. Limit your 'always' and your 'nevers.'"*

> ~ AMY POEHLER, AMERICAN ACTRESS, COMEDIAN,
> VOICE ARTIST, DIRECTOR, PRODUCER, AND WRITER

Stretch your ambition to think of how you can enjoy the pursuit of your career. Think outside of your career box. Many of us are fortunate to have the fantastic opportunity to rebrand our careers at any given time. You have to choose to be career confident and have the courage to try something new. Having an open mind requires effort, follow-through, and analysis of finding out which key will unlock the door that you're determined to open. Your stretch doesn't have to be grand in gesture, but discretionally beneficial to you while finding your place in the evolution of your career.

Action Item of the Day

Ask yourself exactly what do you want your career accomplishments to be and think beyond funding your lifestyle. Write your career story. After reading your completed story, determine specific areas of your life and career that you feel you need to stretch and develop further. Remember that stretching yourself to new levels of excellence should be an ongoing process.

Action List

What is one area that you want to see yourself stretch in professionally?

_____

_____

_____

How will these actions help your career?

_____

_____

_____

Reflections of the day:

Today I accomplished

_____

I learned

_____

I am grateful for

_____

I will invest in

_____

I will repeat

_____

Affirm: I stretch myself to be a more productive professional daily.

Self-Talk Echoes

CAREER AFFIRMATION:

I AM MINDFUL OF THE words that I speak to myself. I choose to speak positively about the professional rock star that I am. I empower myself daily with power-filled words that propel me to consistently make impactful and positive moves.

"Be careful how you are talking to yourself because you are listening."

~ *LISA M. HAYES, LOVE WHISPERER*

Remind yourself to be mindful of self-talk. Be persistent in focusing on the positive of every situation and not permit your words to contradict your actions. Continual positive self-talk is a success habit that can lead to multiple doors of opportunity opening for you. It also repels negative people and surroundings, helps to hush the whisper of doubt, and improves your sentiment about your professional skills and abilities. Monitor what you listen to throughout your day. Choose not to entertain negative communication in all forms. You are capable of creating and undergoing incredible professional experiences. Use your words to frame the positive and impactful career outcomes that you desire to be your reality.

Action Item of the Day

Write seven affirmations that you can recite daily to kick start your positive self-talk conversations. Write your statement in the present tense. Write affirming words that you believe. The words that you speak frame your future.

1. _____

2. _____

3. _____

4. _____

5. _____

6. _____

7. _____

Action List

How would you describe your professional self?

_____

_____

_____

How has the words that you speak of yourself impacted your career to date?

_____

_____

_____

Reflections of the day:

Today I accomplished

_____

I learned

_____

I am grateful for

_____

I will invest in

_____

I will repeat

_____

Affirm: I speak good things about myself and my future.

Embrace Change

CAREER AFFIRMATION:

I CHOOSE TO VIEW MY career path as an adventure. Through all of my career changes, I will be true to myself, my beliefs, and my career goals.

> *"Never let success get to your head; never*
> *let failure get to your heart."*

~ *UNKNOWN*

When changes occur, immediately choose to affirm the work and efforts that you completed—that strengthened your skills, abilities, and overall communication— with a positive attitude and perspective. Take time to identify and honor your growth from your professional lessons. Each professional teaching is an experience that invites you to be grateful of each take-away, valid or challenging. Some associate employment changes with career anxiety. Choose to focus on maximizing each day by reviewing business strategies and best practices. Each learning moment is elevating you to be prepared and ready for the next career level. Be an example of respectful receptiveness to your peers and leadership during the change.

Action Item of the Day

Change is inevitable. Identify what professional best practices and strategies you value and have found most helpful. Have they changed over time? Are you practicing them today? If yes, what changes can be made to make your execution of the methods and strategies more efficient in your life? If no, what is your execution plan to change and re-implement them into your daily routine, if applicable?

Action List

What emotions do you correlate with change? How do they dictate your response to change?

_____

_____

_____

What is your perspective on how the evolution of professional best practices impacts your work performance?

_____

_____

_____

Reflections of the day:

Today I accomplished

_____

I learned

_____

I am grateful for

_____

I will invest in

_____

I will repeat

_____

Affirm: I am open to change, and I respond to change with a positive attitude.

Connect Intentionally

———

CAREER AFFIRMATION:

I AM GRATEFUL FOR THE business relationships that expand the reach of my brand and the impact that I make within my professional community locally and globally.

> *"No partnership between two independent*
> *companies, no matter how well run, can match*
> *the speed, effectiveness, responsiveness and*
> *efficiency of a solely owned company."*

> ~ *EDWARD WHITACRE, JR, FORMER CHAIRMAN*
> *& CEO OF GENERAL MOTORS*

There is no need to be a one-person-army when building your business. Generate synergy, demonstrate trust, and connect with other forward-thinking professionals who together can maximize your business footprint. Today I encourage you to shift out of your comfort zone and maximize your business relationships by developing partnerships from different aspects. Stretch yourself to be open to different opinions and seek brand feedback from colleagues who you respect. Consider creating a product campaign that is mutually beneficial to both businesses.

Activity of the Day

The statement, "We are the average of the five people we spend the most time with" is good food for thought shared by Jim Rohn, an American Entrepreneur, Author and Motivational Speaker.

Write down and analyze who is in your professional inner circle. Your professional inner circle could consist of current or past colleagues, mentors, and current or previous managers.

Action List

What determining factors confirmed who was welcomed and who belonged in your inner circle?

_____

_____

_____

What do you contribute to your inner circle, and what does your inner circle contribute to you?

_____

_____

_____

Reflections of the day:

Today I accomplished

_____

I learned

_____

I am grateful for

_____

I will invest in

_____

I will repeat

_____

Affirm: My inner circle is a safe place and breeds prosperity.

Dear Professional of Success,

Congratulations on completing the *Confidently You, 21-Day Action Plan to Being Your Professional Best.* Repeat these action plans as often needed. Becoming a professional is a journey. Recognize that some areas of your ongoing professional development can take more time than others to witness the growth and improvement. Don't forget to celebrate your wins and appreciate your lessons. Your career relationships and outcomes are a part of your personal legacy. You are worthy and capable to accomplish your career goals and aspirations. Enjoy the journey!

Cheers to becoming the best *Confidently You!*

Michele Badie

Michele Badie, Career Confidence Coach, Blogger, & Podcaster

Let's connect at careertipper.com.

Answer Keys

Page 87

Page 54

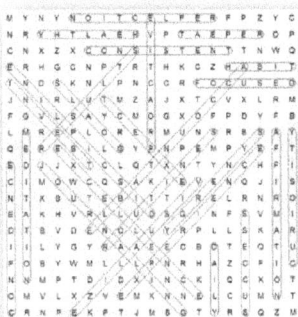

Page 106

www.ingramcontent.com/pod-product-compliance
Lightning Source LLC
Chambersburg PA
CBHW072350090426
42741CB00012B/2994